SEVEN KEYS TO A PEACEFUL PASSING

A Hospice Nurse's Step-by-Step Guide to Hospice

Derek J. Flores, RN

First Edition, April 2018

ISBN: 978-1-7322424-0-1

Dedication

To my mom, Cris—your love, belief in me, and support have made me the man I am today.

I love you!

Table of Contents

Prologue

A few years ago, a person asked me "What's your Dream Job?"

I replied, "I'm doing it!"

Besides being a parent, I believe being a Hospice Nurse is the most rewarding and impactful role I've had in my life. It's not a job, it's a Vocation. A Vocation is more than a job, it's part of who you are at your core. It is what you were meant to be. My Vocation is being a Hospice Nurse.

Let me introduce you to Hospice Care by telling you a short story of two men I knew.

Michael, a man who had just reached the age of 80 was a successful corporate computer executive who had a beautiful family and had lived an unbelievable life. He had made all the right decisions in his youth and throughout his life. Paul hadn't. Paul, a man in his late 70s had a rough life, with failed marriages, lost houses, and no children in his daily life. He had been alone for many years. I had the opportunity to be the Hospice Nurse for both men during the same period of time.

When I arrived at Michael's home, which was in one of Denver's most exclusive neighborhoods I was greeted by an actual guard and other staff caring for the large yard. Conversely, Paul didn't really own anything. He was new to his home, having just moved from Arizona to live with his younger sister and her husband. The couple had created a beautifully decorated room for him with a large window that had a beautiful view of the Colorado Mountains.

Working with both men was an amazing experience for me because of the perspective comparing the two provided on life. One man was arguably what today's society tells us we should strive to be and the other was not. The irony is they both found themselves in identical situations. They were going to die soon.

On the face of it, neither had much in common with each other, but as time went on, I learned they both were Korean War Veterans. I was touched by knowing these two men for more than a few reasons. The first was they reminded me of people I had known over the years, mostly the men who had been influential in my life — my teachers, uncles, coaches, and bosses over the years. They each reminded me of my dad and his buddies. What a wonderful generation!

What hit me the most is the fact we all end up in the same spot at the end of our life. You can make all the right decisions or you can make a series of what the world considers 'mistakes' but death remains a constant. I think it is amazing we all still have the chance to leave this world with dignity, love, and respect. Both Paul and Michael were loved by family and friends in their last days. Michael had the benefit of these relationships for all of his life; Paul had them brought back in his last days. It was a good ending for both men and Hospice had a chance to play a small part in their stories. This is why I chose Hospice as my Vocation.

Introduction

There is no greater gift I have seen than the devotion friends and family have shown for a loved one who is at the end of their life journey. My first encounter with this amazing compassion was the care and love my own grandparents received from my family.

I was blessed to have four living grandparents for the majority of my life. All four lived fairly long lives with the youngest dying in his early 80s and the oldest passing at 103 just a few years ago. The devotion and kindness I witnessed from my parents, as well as their siblings, was amazing. It inspired me and set the course for my own vocation. It wasn't easy for my family to care for aging parents. Their endurance was tested by doing this for many years. My Grandma Rita lived well past her 100th birthday. She had lived an amazing life which encompassed personal joy, tragedy and witnessing the unbelievable progress in daily life created by technology and social change. When she was finally called Home, it was a sad time, but also one of relief. My mom and I had joked about whether grandma would outlive us all. She was a strong and beautiful person.

Having the opportunity and privilege to be a small part of a person's life story is an amazing experience. I am forever changed by my five years in hospice. My hope is this book will empower the reader by transferring a portion of my knowledge and experience for the purpose of reaching their "End of Life Goals". I also hope this effort in writing touches your heart in some way.

Who is this book written for? It's for anyone and everyone who has recently encountered the idea of hospice. Maybe you want more information about hospice for the benefit of a family member of a friend who is ill. Perhaps you've received this book as a gift from someone who knows your heart is hurting because someone you love is very sick and you just want to understand what they are going through. It may be you are a nurse or nursing student considering hospice as your vocation and you want to learn the basics.

The most important reader of this book is someone who has just been told they don't have long to live. My focus is to honor you and what is going on in your life through this transfer of knowledge. I am hopeful it will benefit you and your loved ones in more than one way as you embark on this journey. Peace be with you.

This text leverages my years of work as a Hospice Nurse to benefit people approaching death by empowering them, their friends, family members and caregivers with specific knowledge and inside information about how hospice works as well as specific language you can use to get the best "Hospice Outcome" for yourself or your loved one. Hospice is a human organization with many different moving pieces, quite often operating in an environment of rules and regulations required by the payers of hospice care. This book is a road map to navigate this complex and foreign situation.

In my preparation for writing *Seven Keys to a Peaceful Passing*, I noticed most of the books written by other Hospice Nurses are very heartfelt and sincere. This mirrors how we all practice nursing with our hospice patients. Hospice Nurses have big hearts! Their books are filled with personal stories about the lives and illnesses of amazing patients. What was largely missing from these books was practical advice on getting the best result for the hospice patient. Although I will share some wonderful stories with you, the emphasis of *Seven Keys to a Peaceful Passing* is to provide a down-to-earth resource. You will learn how the hospice system works, so you can maintain your focus on what really matters to you.

My inspiration for writing this book occurred while helping a dear friend whose mother was dying of cancer. Jon and I have been buddies since rooming together at Colorado State University. Jon was trying to contribute to his family's efforts to care for his mother but lived far away from them. He had visited his mom recently but still wanted to be part of the effort to care for her. We spoke a few times over coffee about his mother's illness — then one day Jon called me with urgency asking for help.

His mom was reporting pain which was not being controlled despite multiple visits from her Hospice Team. On the surface, it sounded as if the hospice staff was not addressing her needs, but it was more complicated than that. His parents had been independent people all their lives and Jon's elderly father wanted to continue to care for his beloved wife to maintain their privacy and independence. For whatever reason, things weren't working. Jon's mom needed her pain controlled! During our conversation, I gave Jon two phrases which I knew would instantly get the attention of the Hospice Team caring for his mother. It worked! By the end of the day, her pain was under control and everyone caring for her was on the same page. I hadn't offered any nursing advice or chosen a new medication or dosage. Instead, I suggested words and phrases which I knew would grab the attention of the Hospice Team in Georgia.

Knowledge and words can be so powerful!

Before I start the discussion, a few housekeeping items. One principle I have always applied as a nurse is maintaining the dignity of my patients. Every nurse I know does the same thing. In writing this book, it was difficult to maintain the language to identify who I was speaking about without compromising a simple identifier. Please forgive me for referring to a person as "patient". This word patient can seem antiseptic and impersonal, but it is unique and necessary to identify who I am writing about.

This book will not provide medical or nursing advice for your particular situation. Rather, I am providing information on how hospice care works in general. Individual patient care decisions should be made in cooperation with your Hospice Team who will provide you with specific recommendations based on your unique situation.

The personal stories included here have been altered to maintain the personal privacy of any person and are also composites of multiple cases over the years.

Chapter One

What Hospice Is & Isn't?

My best description of hospice:

"A team of healthcare and psychosocial professionals working together to provide the best end of life experience for the patient and their family by helping meet the goals established at the start of hospice care."

One thing which amazes me in any discussion of End of Life Care is how often people just don't understand what hospice care really is. The average person doesn't think about death or dying on a regular basis. Why would they? Death is usually only something we deal with when the circumstances of life force it on us. Even then, it isn't easy to think or talk about.

Perhaps this is the situation you find yourself in. So, let's bring you up to speed on the basics of hospice. The purpose of hospice is simply to meet the medical, spiritual, and emotional needs of a terminally ill person. The term "terminal" describes a situation where a doctor has given a diagnosis which will likely result in death within six months. The weight of this word on a person's psyche and spirit can be very heavy. Each diagnosis is different in what it really means to a patient and family. For someone with pancreatic cancer, it may mean a rush to get one's affairs in order because of the rapid pace of this disease. For someone with Alzheimer's, it may mean the long journey for patient and family is coming to an end. No matter what your situation is, the word "terminal" is significant and important.

Quite often in the discussion of a terminal disease or diagnosis, the term "Comfort Care" is introduced. What is Comfort Care? It is really based on a simple wish for the person who is dying to have a painless and distress-free passing. Pain and distress may come in a variety of forms including physical, mental, emotional or spiritual. All the resources and assets of the hospice organization are focused on providing Comfort Care for its patients. Hospice is a blend of medical, psychosocial, and spiritual care intended to meet the patient's needs while supporting their family through this most difficult of times.

During the thousands of discussions I've had with patients and their family members, there was an array of reactions and perceptions of what they thought about hospice was. Sometimes people experienced fear, thinking hospice was a "Death Sentence" for them. They would sometimes verbalize they had no hope. This can be heartbreaking. However, the reality is most new patients and caregivers experienced a feeling of relief that more professional care, resources, and equipment were available because they were utilizing hospice.

A little-known fact is some people "graduate" from hospice. Patients can thrive on the combination of professional care, combined with the existing care they receive from their family and caregivers. Often, the improvement in a hospice patient's condition is evidenced by various improvements such as an increase in body weight or the successful management of symptoms which have been achieved because of adjustments to a medication regimen.

Is Hospice a Place?

People often think Hospice is a physical facility where patients are cared for and is owned and run by a hospice organization. Most of the time it is not. Hospice organizations go to wherever their patients reside. Patients may be living in their own home, with an adult child, at a nursing or assisted living facility. Even a hospital.

Ideally, most of us would choose to be in our home for the last days of our life. Being at home is the first choice for many patients and families. As long as there isn't a symptom management reason or safety issue with the house, this can happen if the Hospice Team and family work together. There are actually few situations where someone can't be cared for at home. Conditions which make caring for someone to be at home difficult include Alzheimer's or Dementia in patients who are still able to walk. Another complication to at home care is a lack of multiple caregivers available to provide care around the clock in the patient's home.

A small portion of hospice patients receive care in "brick and mortar" facilities. This type of facility is usually provided by a larger Hospice organization with the resources to staff it 24/7. Staff at any of these facilities often include doctors, nurses and nursing assistants as well as social workers and chaplains available to help patients and their families. Standalone Hospice facilities are often found in larger metropolitan areas. Only a hospice which cares for a large number of patients at one time can afford to provide staff and facilities like this. Usually, only patients who are having trouble with managing symptoms such as pain or shortness of breath need to use these types of facilities. I will be discussing the different "Levels of Care" in the next section. Nursing Homes and other facilities are not usually utilized by the average patient.

Levels of Care

To understand hospice care requires the knowledge of the different levels of care provided by hospice. There are four levels of care provided by hospice as part of the Medicare Benefit: GIP, Routine, Continuous, and Respite.

General Inpatient Care (GIP) is provided in an inpatient facility such at a hospital or nursing home where there is a cooperative effort between the facility and the hospice. A hospice organization may even form a cooperative partnership to provide GIP Care with a nursing home or hospital where there is an already a 24/7 nursing team in place. In these situations, the nursing staffs in hospitals and nursing homes work together with Hospice Nurses to provide care for the patient.

My own experiences with GIP care usually began with a phone call before I started my shift saying I had a new patient who needed to be evaluated for the GIP Level of Care. Then the process ended with me both admitting the patient and attending their death a few hours later. This type of scenario is often a roller coaster of emotions for everyone involved. Patients in GIP Level of Care were the most challenging and rewarding patients to work with.

The vast majority of hospice patients don't need this level of care because they do not meet the requirements for General Inpatient Care (GIP). Qualifications for GIP include, but are not limited to uncontrolled symptoms such as pain or shortness of breath. The main qualifier is that care cannot be managed where the patient resides. Check with your Hospice Team on the specifics of GIP Care to see if your situation qualifies.

The Routine Level of Care is what most hospice patients receive. Patients on the Routine Level of Care may live in one of a few places—an assisted living facility, or, quite often, the person's own residence. Nursing homes also provide Routine Level of Care, which is different from the GIP Level of Care described earlier. Hospice Patients who live in nursing homes often have had a decline in their condition which requires care above and beyond what the caregivers or family can provide at home.

One of the most heartbreaking and frustrating situations I ran into as a Hospice Nurse was working with a patient and family who were trying to fulfill a promise they made to their elderly parent about "never being placed in a nursing home". I can certainly understand this. Sometimes the facts of a situation are overwhelming. I have had dozens of patients over the years who had lived in their own homes for decades, then were moved to a nursing home facility. Quite often the result was good. When a family member becomes a full-time caregiver for a parent, they sometimes lose some of their identity as a child of the patient. They are often exhausted and at risk of becoming ill themselves. The move from home to a nursing home can restore the parent-child relationship by removing the overwhelming burden of providing 24/7 care for an aging parent.

Additionally, keeping a patient at home may create real risk for injury. Unfortunately, a patient may begin to fall on a regular basis, which can be a result of suffering from dementia or Alzheimer's. It simply may not be a safe situation anymore for the patient.

Hospice Nurses and Social Workers can suggest

a change in living location for a patient, but we can't make the decision to move a patient to a nursing home. Only the person with legal authority can make this decision. One worst case situation we all want to avoid is a patient who has fallen in their home in the middle of the night and has stayed on the floor for an extended period of time.

Other reasons for moving someone from home to a facility include "Caregiver Breakdown", which is a description of a person or persons who are caring for an ill person to their own detriment. Quite often, the person providing care is older also. The stresses and strains of providing such care are real. It is important to take care of yourself as well as loved ones. Every person's and every family's situation is different. My suggestion is to not wait to make a decision to move your loved one from a home to a facility which may truly benefit them. There are also other options to help keep a person safely at home, which will be discussed in a later chapter.

Continuous Care is the next "Level of Care" we will discuss. It involves taking care of a patient around the clock in an effort to control symptoms such as severe pain, nausea, terminal agitation, bleeding, acute respiratory distress, or change in level of consciousness. This 8 to 24 hour care period has to be predominantly provided by a Skilled Nurse. The term Skilled Nurse refers to either a Registered Nurse or LPN. Certified Nursing Assistants can also be part of the Continuous Care Team, just not providing the majority of hours of care each day. If symptoms are being controlled in a patient, then the criteria for this level of care had not been met and it will not be available. Please consult with your Hospice Team for the details of this Level of Care. The "Continuous" Level of Care is not often used, mainly because the patient, family, and even Hospice Team may not be fully aware of its availability and proper application.

'Key' #1 - A Valuable Tool

I will now give you my first 'Key' to a Peaceful Passing while introducing the last of the four Levels of Care. **Hospice is a tool available to make your life easier.** To avoid burnout and maintain the physical, emotional, and spiritual health of the rest of your family, I suggest you consider using the '**Respite' Level of Care**.

Some patients in hospice have been taken care of by the same person or people for an extended period time. This is a wonderful act of kindness on the caregiver's part, but it has probably been very hard on the day-to-day caregivers who are most likely family members. My own family cared for both sets of grandparents for a long period of time, with my maternal grandparents having fifteen years of frequent care by their adult children.

"Respite" level of care is when the patient is moved to a facility for a short period of time to allow caregivers a chance to recuperate. Respite Care normally occurs in a skilled nursing facility within your community. Both your nurse and social worker will work with the rest of the team to determine eligibility and quali-fying facilities who can provide care for your loved one. Respite stays are usually five days long per benefit period.

I understand it may be very difficult to have your parent or loved one go to a skilled nursing facility for temporary care— we all have an emotional involve-ment in providing care for our own family members. But at some point, we reach our physical and emotional limits. It can be beneficial to both patient and caregiver to just get a break and recharge.

Which Facility Is Best?

Oftentimes, a family is caught off-guard by a rapid de-cline in their loved one's condition. Sometimes, a fall or a stroke places difficult decisions in the lap of a fam-ily member who is trying to act based on what they think their loved one would want. These decisions are often rushed.

It is beneficial to take your time to make an in-formed decision. One story I will share repeated itself during my years in hospice. It went something like this: "We were driving to one of the nursing facilities you had on your list where Dad could possibly stay. On the way there we saw this beautiful new facility". We all want what's best for our loved one, but it's important to know that the newness or beauty of a facility does not necessarily correlate to the quality care being provided there. Quite often new buildings also have new staffs. Some of the best facilities I've worked in as a visiting

Hospice Nurse had well-established teams who provided excellent care. These places may have not have the nicest furniture or a personal chef on staff, but the nurses and CNAs provide top notch care. If someone on your Hospice Team gives you a list of facilities they trust, it's important to take time and investigate the real qualities and features of each location.

Another tip is for all of us to share our own wishes about possible locations we would like to use if needed at some time in our lives, so our family does not wonder what our wishes are.

What Hospice is Not

A common misunderstanding between the patient, their family/caregivers, and the hospice company is how often Hospice Team Members will be coming to care for the patient. Hospice can be best be described as "intermittent care", meaning that care will be provided occasionally—not throughout the day and night on a full-time basis under normal circumstances.

Keep in mind there's always someone you can call for help when you are on hospice care, but the day-to-day 24/7 care for a patient's living needs to be provided by someone outside the Hospice Team, such as the friend, caregiver, family member, or facility staff.

People often have the impression their caregiving workload will be greatly reduced when a patient is admitted to hospice care. This misunderstanding happens frequently with families who have been providing care for their loved one at home for an extended period of time. They may be completely exhausted by the time hospice becomes involved. The truth is hospice will make a difference, but it may be in ways you don't expect.

Hospice care will reduce the "overall load" to you and your family by providing assistance with tasks such as biweekly baths or showers, management of medications, and regular nursing visits, etc. Every hospice is slightly different in what they provide, so ask questions about what services are provided when you are interviewing a hospice. Hospice is really meant to supplement what is already being provided. My experience is both families and patients respond to the extra assistance a Hospice Team provides in a positive way.

Another area where misunderstandings can occur is medication. During the admission process to hospice, the admitting nurse and physician will work together to establish a primary diagnosis for the patient. From this primary diagnosis, decisions are made about which medications will be paid for by hospice, which ones are not, and which ones may not be benefiting the patient and should be discontinued. Examples of commonly discontinued medications are vitamins or a drug used in the early stages of Alzheimer's when a person's disease has moved well past the likely benefit of the medication. Medications should always be reviewed for their effectiveness and whether they fit in with the patient's goals for care.

Every family and patient are different in their desire to be involved in medication decisions. If this is very important to you, then verbalize this to the nurse during the admission process. Medications which aren't covered by hospice may be ok to be continued but must be paid by you or another payor source. Sometimes an alternative drug can be used at a lower cost. I suggest keeping the lines of communication open between nurses, doctors, and families during and after the admission process to make sure everyone is on the same page.

Perhaps the most important topic to address in this section is that hospice does not traditionally pay for any curative treatment. What is a curative medication/ treatment? The best example would be something like chemotherapy. Curative drugs and therapies are used in an effort to eliminate a disease or effects of an injury. There can be a myriad of treatments, medications, or imaging such as CT scans, all administered with *the ultimate goal of curing a disease*. Surgery would also be considered a curative treatment. This is not what hospice is traditionally meant to do. Instead, hospice care has been built around the idea of bringing "Comfort Care" to its patients. There may be a few hospice organizations nationwide who deviate from this common practice, but the vast majority of hospices do not offer curative medications or therapies. Those hospices which may be providing curative drugs or therapies are paying for these services out of their own pocket or utilizing a foundation or charitable type funding.

It is important to recognize that patients and families often go through a difficult emotional process when letting go of the treatment, medications, daily routines and often the healthcare team which has been doing everything they can to bring them back to good health. These medical interventions and the people who deliver them are the definition of "Hope" to someone who is very ill and wants to get back to the life they have been living.

A person who has a deadly disease often does everything they can do to stay alive. It is common for the decision to cease curative treatment and go into hospice care to be an emotional one which may involve many people besides the patient themselves. Some loved ones may be asking the terminally ill person to continue treatment in hope of a miracle. The most common scenario in is an adult child lobbying their elderly parent to continue receiving chemo or radiation for metastatic cancer. My anecdotal experience is the family member who wants the patient to continue treatment often lives a great distance away from the patient or they may have had a strained relationship and really want to have more time together. This is totally understandable but may not be in the best interest of the patient.

Decisions on hospice care and the changes it may require can be very difficult for everyone involved. What I observed over the years is that at some point the physical signs of battling a disease like cancer or other conditions become overwhelming, and an emotional tipping point arrives where everyone involved comes to the realization that the end is near. I believe this is a sense built into our human nature—we have a sense of death approaching. This realization is usually followed by the decision to begin hospice care. The battle against a terminal disease is physically, spiritually, and emotionally demanding. Having these burdens released can give everyone involved new energy and joy in being set free from the struggle they have been involved in. This is a healing all in itself.

Who Pays for Hospice?

As with just about everything in our lives, money does play a role in hospice. The vast majority of hospice care is paid for through the Medicare Part A benefit. Because most hospice patients are elderly and qualify for Medicare, issues related to payment are few and far between.

Payment for hospice services can be more challenging when the person receiving care is not elderly and does not qualify for Medicare. Younger people who are in hospice are usually cancer patients, so the expertise of the Hospice Social Worker as well as the administration staff is essential. Private Health Insurance companies also pay for hospice care for some patients, each having different requirements and benefit packages. If you fall into this category, talk with your Hospice Team about your options. I've never seen a situation where the care of a person has been refused by a hospice because of payment. If a payor source could not be secured, the hospice always stepped up to say it would be gratis—no fee to the patient. I am not making a promise to you here, but I believe Hospice organizations at their core have always been run by people who are concerned for their fellow man.

Chapter Two

The Hospice Team

Like any other team, a hospice organization has multiple players with unique roles. In this section, I'll discuss the education, experience, typical job description, and role of each member, as well as provide insider tips on how to create the best working relationship with each team member.

Every hospice organization usually has a slightly different mix of disciplines working together, for example, not every hospice has a Music Therapist. Instead, they may employ a person in another position.

The Liaison

Most likely the first person you will encounter on a Hospice Team is the person responsible for bringing new patients into hospice care. The word used to describe how many patients are being taken care of by an individual hospice organization is "census". Hospice Liaisons always know what their census is.

Liaisons come from varied backgrounds. Sometimes they are business people with a background in the medical field. Others are social workers or nurses who have decided they want to play a different role on the Hospice Team. These folks may have different titles, such as marketing coordinator, or patient advisor. They are empathetic and compassionate people who help educate and coordinate often complicated situations.

Liaisons invest time and effort into their business relationships with a variety of contacts in the healthcare world. They assist and network with hospitals, physician groups, nursing homes, assisted living facilities, and any other people and facilities where new patients may come from.

Liaisons are in the difficult position of having to market the hospice by differentiating it from competitors. Each hospice normally has its own niche—the thing they are known for. Sometimes it is having a great nursing staff, an inpatient facility, well-respected doctors, excellent customer service, or great volunteers as part of their team.

Usually, the Hospice Team who responds quickly to new patient needs and provides excellent care is the hospice who wins referrals from doctors and facility staff. Most hospices should be able to evaluate a new patient within a few hours of being called by the referring source. If you are told you need to wait longer than this, consider picking up the phone and finding another hospice. The only exception to this would be a rural-based hospice, but even then, no one should wait an unreasonable amount of time to be evaluated. Their response time to your initial visit may be reflective of how long you have to wait for other services once you are a patient in their care.

New patients are often admitted to hospice care during very trying times for everyone involved. Liaisons are kind people who are well briefed on their organization's services and staff backgrounds. Ask them to tell you about the accreditations and experience of the professionals providing your care.

I have found the best liaisons are ones who have long-standing relationships with the people and facilities they serve. They won't over-promise and they stay involved with achieving patient and family goals throughout the entire hospice journey.

The Nurses

There are multiple nurses on staff in most hospice organizations. The RN Case Manager (RNCM) is most often the lead team member. I have heard in some places a social worker may fill the role of Case Manager, but I have never personally seen it happen. Registered Nurses (RNs) are professionals who have at least two years of intense education and training at an accredited school. Some RNs have an associate's degree called an ADN or Associates Degree in Nursing. Others have a bachelor's degree in nursing from a four-year institution. Both educational pathways produce great nurses. The difference in some settings is a person with a BSN (Bachelors of Nursing) has had to take courses qualifying them for leadership and management positions in healthcare. The current trend in nursing, especially among hospitals, is to only hire BSNs.

Nurses who have graduated from nursing school are not legally nurses until two things occur after graduation. The first is successful passage of the NCLEX Exam (National Council Licensure Examination). This is a very difficult exam which is given all over the U.S. If a person passes the NCLEX exam, they then submit an application for licensure in their state. Only after meeting the criteria of the applicable state, which includes a background check, is a nursing license issued. Depending on which state or territory you are in, you may or may not have an LPN or Practical Nurse on your Hospice Team. They do perform many of the same tasks as an RN but have limitations on their role. In Colorado, LPNs are common in Skilled Nursing Facilities a.k.a. Nursing Homes. They do amazing work in often difficult situations around the clock.

RNCMs usually visit their patients once or twice a week to do a nursing assessment. Most visits last between thirty and sixty minutes. The frequency and length of visits can depend on whether symptoms are being actively managed, or the minimum number of visits may be dictated by company policy. Hospice Nurses are experts in pain management—this is their most visible role on the team. By coordinating medications under the direction of a physicia able to get and keep a patient comfortable.

What makes a good nurse? It's something called nursing judgment. It's a trait us nurses take to heart. Nursing judgment is a combination of knowledge, intellect, and experience. It's knowing when a patient is headed for trouble and making the right decisions to avoid a crisis.

On-Call

A less visible, but just as important, role is the On-Call Nurses These nurses are most often Registered Nurses, with the same education and licensing required as any other RN.

The role of working On-call is the position in hospice I spent the most time in. The work is usually "feast or famine". I could spend an entire work night at home without any patient visits and then be out all night the next evening seeing multiple patients spread out over a 50 mile radius. It is a tiring and rewarding position.

The schedule for On-Call Nurses varies in each hospice organization. Most often, it depends on the number of patients being served as well as the total number of nurses on staff. Besides providing the necessary nursing care, the on-call nurse provides relief for the RN Case Managers who put in very long days during the week. Nothing burns out a nursing staff and creates turn-over quicker than RN Case Managers having to work on-call shifts during the week after the normal work day—that means having to work 32 hours straight.

On-Call RN's are the nurses you will most often encounter on weekends and after hours during the week. They can't be heavy sleepers, as their phones are kept next to their beds and they need to be out the door quickly to see a patient who may be struggling with pain or another symptom such as shortness of breath.

The Hospice Physician

Every hospice has a Medical Director who is a physician. Physicians go through study, internship, and residency often lasting over a decade, depending on their specialty and credentials. New doctors are often in their thirties before they begin to earn a living and are often well over six figures in Student Loan Debt when they settle into their first real job. Doctors have sacrificed a lot to care for those in need, especially in the current healthcare insurance environment. The days of doctors making huge incomes with moderate an effort are over.

Just as in any profession, there are variations in the experience and qualifications of a Hospice Physician. Hospices employ both M.D.'s and D.O.'s, who have nearly identical training and accreditation Depending on the census. Individual hospices may or may not have resources for more than one physician. Also of note are the high achievements physicians make in their fellowship and board certifications.

Hospice Physicians are an essential part of any hospice organization.

Attending Physicians

One of the first decisions a new patient and their family need to make when beginning hospice services is who will act as the "Attending Physician". The Attending Physician is the person who takes responsibility for the patient's day-to-day medical decisions. They work with nurses and the other members of the team, issue medication orders, and evaluate recertifications. Doctors also take on-call shifts by being available overnight to address patient needs. I am always impressed by the great majority of doctors who answer the phone in the middle of the night with what must be a smile. They are big-hearted people who add much to the Hospice Team.

Sometimes the patient's Primary Care Physician (PCP) will request to follow their patient and act as the Attending Physician. Other times, the PCP will defer to the Hospice Physician to also act as the Attending Physician. It all depends on the individual doctors involved. There is no requirement or standard for who will act as the Attending. I would suggest that if your PCP wants to act as your Attending Physician, to ask them how much experience they have in symptom management of Hospice Patients. Having a doctor who can give sound direction to the Hospice Team is essential for a good hospice outcome.

How do doctors work within a hospice organization? There are many tasks a Hospice Doctor is responsible for. Most important is working with the nurse who is at the patient's bedside managing symptoms. Practically, this means the nurse calls the physician after conducting an assessment where a problem is observed to discuss the situation and what should be done next.

Doctors who work in hospice care are usually also employed by at least one other organization, it could be a gerontology practice, but possibly in a hospital, clinic, or other type of practice such as a group of doctors who visit patients in their homes. The only place you don't usually see them working is with another hospice. This unwritten rule is unique to the hospice world. Whether you are a CNA, nurse, or doctor, working for two or more hospices is seen as a conflict of interest.

The role of a physician may vary depending on the hospice. In a smaller hospice, usually with a census of seventy-five patients or less, the doctor may wear many hats including Medical Director. Doctors usually conduct face-to-face visits for people who need to be admitted to hospice if that person has had hospice care before. They also see patients in-person during certain recertification periods.

When entering hospice, a new patient comes with a 90 day benefit period. This means that for the first 90 days, there is no recertification paperwork needed to be completed by the Hospice Team. After that 90 day window, each of the team members needs to make a visit with the patient and fill out the required paperwork reporting the condition of the patient. This process helps determine whether the patient will continue to qualify for hospice care. The first 90 day Medicare period is followed by another 90 day period, then there are 60 day periods between recertifications after that.

One of the most important roles of a physician in hospice care is participation in a bi-weekly meeting often called IDT or Interdisciplinary Team Meeting. During these meetings, which are usually held in the middle of the week, physicians review orders for medications as well as reviewing and endorsing recertification paperwork and other housekeeping tasks.

Technology plays an important part in the communication between doctors, nurses, and pharmacies. Especially in the middle of the night. If your Primary Care Physician wants to act as your Attending Physician, they and their practice colleagues should have the ability to fax prescriptions to a pharmacy. There is nothing more important to a hospice patient who needs important medications than getting them quickly. If your PCP has decided to follow as the Attending Physician, then knowing if they and their On-Call Physicians have this capability is very important. Pharmacies are under increasing pressure by the government to make sure their medication orders are authentic and accurate, so having a doctor who can use technology to quickly send a prescription can make the difference between having a symptom like pain treated promptly and having to wait. This tip may seem to be a little "in the weeds", but I've had patients wait for important medication because the On-Call Physician couldn't fax from their location.

The Pharmacist

An often overlooked member of the Hospice Team is the pharmacist. Unless you are working with a larger hospice, they probably don't have a full-time pharmacist on staff. Instead, your hospice may work with a pharmacy that works with more than one hospice at a time.

The knowledge of a pharmacist who is experienced in hospice care is invaluable. The history of pharmacy goes back eons. Pharmacy can often require being creative in treating certain symptoms.

It is a little known fact that there are pharmacists around the country who still compound medications. This skill can benefit a patient who perhaps has not had a particular symptom controlled, such as nausea. Compounding is becoming a lost art. All pharmacists had this skill and practiced daily a century ago. The standard pharmacy seems to work for 90% of patients and their issues, the other 10% may need something creative to help solve an immediate problem. A pharmacist who can construct creams and lotions for external applications can bring relief to someone who has been struggling. Hospice pharmacists will work with the nurse and physician on difficult cases to control symptoms which are expected and anticipate the unexpected situations.

If you or your loved one are searching for a hospice provider, knowing their arrangement with an experienced pharmacist can be very important to achieving a peaceful passing. This is especially important for those who have an unusual diagnosis such as ALS also known as Lou Gehrig's Disease or with symptoms which may not have been successfully treated up to the time of hospice admission.

Other times, the most important issue related to a pharmacist is the speed at which prescriptions can be filled. Many crisis which occur in hospice seem to happen in the middle of the night, so asking up front how a Hospice Team will deal with getting needed medications which are not on hand is important. Having a loved one in pain for multiple hours because the nearest pharmacy which is open at 3 am is 30 miles away is not good for anyone.

Most medications in hospice are given orally, but sometimes circumstances require they be given subcutaneously or intravenously via an electronic pump. This is uncommon but does happen. If it is needed, a special pharmacy will likely get involved to supply the medication, equipment, and may be needed to initiate the medication. Sometimes a special infusion nurse may come to get everything started.

The Chaplain

A non-denominational chaplain is an integral part of a Hospice Team. This person is often an ordained minister who usually has years of seminary studies in addition to a four-year degree from a college or university. Chaplains are often men and women who are from a Protestant Christian denomination. There is also an abundance of former Catholic Priests who are often not allowed to publicly act as priests by their local Catholic Bishop, but do know what Catholics believe and will pray with you. These men have kind and caring hearts. They can also contact the local Catholic Parish on your behalf to facilitate a 'Licit' administration of all the Catholic Sacraments.

Chaplains visit patients less frequently than other team members, sometimes bi-weekly or monthly. If you would like more frequent visits, they can often meet this need. From time to time, I have heard patients express hesitation about working with a chaplain. They are concerned that the chaplain may be on some sort of mission to convert or "save" the patient before they die. I've never seen this happen. Patients are very emotionally vulnerable at this point in their lives, so everyone involved in their care is tasked with accepting their patients as they are.

Atheism, agnosticism, and secularism are becoming more prevalent these days. Some people also consider themselves spiritual but do not identify with a particular faith tradition. I have found that chaplains take people where they are in their spiritual journey. Chaplains offer emotional and spiritual support combined with kindness and patience. They also play an important role in helping a person perform a 'life review', which is a therapeutic way to find peace in talking about events and experiences. If you don't want a chaplain because you don't believe in God, they will gladly set aside discussion of faith and just be a friend who wants to be there for you to listen and provide counsel from a secular perspective. If you are unsure about working with a chaplain, I would encourage you to try it for one or two visits and see if you "click".

The Social Worker

Another integral professional on the Hospice Team is the Social Worker. Social Workers have many years of higher education. After obtaining a four-year bachelor's degree, some Social Workers enter the workforce, but most earn a Master's of Social Work Degree (MSW) first. The advanced degree is almost necessary to earn a livable income. In addition, each state has licensure requirements which may include internships. Social Workers are often in salaried positions where they are expected to take care of patient needs, even if this extends well past the traditional work day which includes on-call shifts, nights, and weekends. Social Workers have huge hearts for their patients and are amazingly devoted!

Quite often there is only one Social Worker on staff with each hospice. They have the task of seeing everyone. This means assessing new patients and seeing all their regular patients on a regular schedule. A Social Worker is often the miracle worker who eliminates what often seems like an impossible financial or caretaking dilemma.

Social Workers in hospice care wear many hats. Besides needing to know all the ins and outs of the financial and benefits side of hospice, they regularly are the emotional crutch for everyone else. I've always been amazed at the ability of a social worker to be emotionally present for patients and family members who are grieving, then see them an hour later coordinating a meeting for another family in a completely different situation. Social workers are often the person other Hospice Team Members turn to when they are having difficulty processing their own grief. I don't know how they do it.

The CNA

I believe the most important person in the Hospice Team is the Certified Nursing Assistant, also known as the CNA. These amazing folks are licensed after completing a required course of study. CNAs are quite frankly underpaid and often overworked! They have the most personal interaction with patients and families. This enables them to make observations about changes in the condition of their patients. They provide invaluable information.

Before becoming a nurse, I worked as a CNA in Home Health for two years. These years of working and studying formed my perspective on the daily struggles patients face. CNA's help with the Activities of Daily Living, also known as ADLs. CNA's aid with tasks such as showering, meal preparation, changing bed linen, and other tasks the patient cannot complete alone.

Being a CNA requires a big heart, an eye for detail, and the ability to observe small changes in patients. A good CNA is worth their weight in gold because the information they pass on to the nurse can make the difference between a patient being in distress and quick and effective symptom management by the nurse and doctor. CNAs generally make two visits with each of their patients each week.

The best way you can assist your CNA is to communicate well with them. They are usually on a tight schedule throughout their day. If you are running low on supplies, then please ask them for more before they arrive at your home or while they are there. It will save them an extra trip.

Here's a little-known fact. All licensed medical professionals operate under what is called a "Scope of Practice". This is basically a list of what they can and cannot do. There is often a temptation for families to ask CNA's to do more than they are allowed to, things like administer a medication or change a wound dressing they have not been authorized to. This may be convenient in the moment, but it may cause big problems for the CNA including dismissal and loss of license.

The Administrator

If there is a role in hospice which rarely gets any accolades, it's the person who plays the role of Administrator during weekends and weekday nights. They are often the leader of the On-Call Team. This person may be a social worker, nurse, nurse manager, or office manager during the regular business week. The role of Administrator is important in helping the other team members who work on nights and weekends. The Administrator will review initial information about whether a patient has a hospice insurance benefit as well as any other patient need which must be addressed. New patient admissions are a big part of most weekends and the Administrator often coordinates the delivery of needed equipment such as hospital beds and other equipment.

The Owner or Director

Probably the one person who you will never talk to, but who makes the biggest impact on the quality of hospice care, is the owner or Director. This person sets the tone and vision for their hospice, setting long-range goals as well as dealing with day-to-day challenges like any business owner/general manager. If you have a compliment or concern to share about your hospice experience, the owner of a hospice would be grateful for the feedback.

Hospice Volunteers

Another important team member in Hospice is the Volunteer. They are kind-hearted people from your community who offer their own personal time to spend with hospice patients. Quite often the nurse and sometimes the CNA are being pulled in many different directions during their workday. Volunteers are not.

They can spend special one-on-one time with patients and their families, providing emotional support and friendship. Unfortunately, not every hospice has an abundance of volunteers. If you would like a volunteer to spend time with your loved one, ask your RNCM or any other team member if one is available. If you are a caregiver, I hope you will consider being a volunteer yourself when this hospice journey is over.

The best way to thank a volunteer or any Hospice Team Member is a simple, "thank you". Offering gifts of any type puts a Hospice Team Member in a difficult position. Hospice organizations want to make sure the patient—staff relationships are not compromised in any way. A staff member receiving a gift from a family could lead to their termination.

Chapter Three
Choosing a Hospice

In some metropolitan areas, there are literally dozens of hospice organizations. With such intense competition for patients, each organization is vying for an edge to become your hospice of choice. There are both Profit and Not-For-Profit entities providing hospice care in the U.S. I have worked for both. A whole book could be written on the differences between the two. My experience is that all my patients received everything they needed with either, so I will not delve into this topic.

When comparing hospice organizations, there are many things to consider. Like any other enterprise, their financial status and resources are important. For the sake of discussion, let's assume each hospice you are considering is working with roughly the same number of dollars per patient per day from Medicare and other payor sources. The only real financial differences difference is likely the age of their hospice organization. Some hospices have been around for decades and during this time, they may have accumulated cash reserves which enable them to do things new organizations cannot do.

The history of a hospice's management of finances over time is important. A few years ago in Colorado, a large hospice went out of business in part because they had mismanaged funds by throwing extravagant parties. Another local hospice created a public relation nightmare for themselves by paying upper management outrageous salaries. Both organizations had their dirty laundry discovered by local newspapers. A simple Google search should reveal any dubious behavior going on with a hospice you are considering. Also, asking contacts and friends you know in the healthcare field about your prospective choices can provide good information.

There are other things to consider. Sometimes, a hospice provides one of the disciplines (Nurse, CNA, etc.) more frequently, with others possibly coming to visit less often. In some cases, a hospice provides a special service, such as music or pet therapy. Every hospice in your area wants to differentiate themselves in some way or another.

Instead of using these bells and whistles to choose a hospice, I would suggest digging deeper to learn more about the tenure of the staff and whether any of their nurses are endorsed as Certified Hospice and Palliative Nurse (CHPN) or if there their doctors have earned the designation by the Hospice Medical Director Certification Board (HMDCB), a designation earned by physicians through an exam. These achievements are evidence of special skills and knowledge which may benefit you.

As you can tell, choosing a hospice organization to work with can be a complex task. I would suggest approaching it as you would any other major purchasing decision. Ask questions, collect information and trust your instincts in making the best choice for your unique situation.

One way you can go a little deeper in your search for an excellent hospice is to tell the Hospice Liaison you are interviewing that you wish to meet the Registered Nurse Case Manager who would be providing care for the patient. Meeting this nurse and even the CNA can help make an educated and informed decision about which hospice is the right fit for you. Most nurses can make themselves available for 15 minutes to say hello to you.

"Key" #2 - A Load off Your Mind

Make sure that the RNCM you are working with seems capable of taking on another patient—they are there to take some of the load off of you, knowing how much they can really lift off your shoulders is important.

Being a Hospice Nurse is not easy, especially for the RN Case Managers. They are almost constantly being pulled in many different directions at the same time. Quite often, the time they spend with patients feels like anything but work—it's a break from paperwork and meetings. Some people have described the role of RNCM as an "impossible job". It's not impossible, but it does require a level of dedication which is more often than not compatible with having a normal life outside of work. RNCMs usually put in long days, then come home and spend hours completing paperwork. This schedule is very hard to sustain over an extended period of time and a high turnover rate for RNCM's is a major concern for most hospices. Also of note is your RNCM's patient load. Knowing whether you or your loved one are going to be one of ten patients or one of eighteen patients being taken care of by a particular RNCM is important. Having this knowledge before you choose a hospice is more valuable than after.

Chapter Four
A Hospice Journey
–
Step by Step

You are about to embark on a major task. Half the anxiousness of any new situation comes from not knowing what to expect. Let me lay out the most common timeline you may encounter in your hospice journey. Hopefully, it benefits you and takes away those "what's next" moments. This is the most common chronology of hospice care today—your hospice and particular situation may occur differently.

The Consultation

The first step towards Hospice usually begins with a discussion between a patient and their doctor. Perhaps it is an oncologist speaking with a longtime patient who has run out of chemotherapy, surgical, or radiation options. Maybe it is an emergency room physician who is talking to a large extended family whose grandfather has just suffered a devastating stroke. No matter the details of how you arrive at this moment, hearing tragic news is never pleasant.

Most hospitals and facilities will offer a list of local hospice providers to the person who is able to make decisions. This may be the patient themselves, or it may be a family member or friend who has legal authority to do so. The idea of giving a list of more than one hospice is in the interest of being fair, so the doctor, social worker or hospital discharge planner isn't promoting a particular hospice. Your decision in choosing a hospice is very important, please interview at least a few different hospices, and then choose the one you feel most comfortable with.

Signing up for hospice care is very easy. Usually the Hospice Liaison, but sometimes a different Hospice Team Member will explain the process, ask you to review the information with them, and then have you sign a few forms authorizing the patient to be evaluated for hospice care. Once a hospice organization has been chosen and consents have been signed, you can expect many visitors to your home over the following week. It is very important for you to know that not every person who signs up for hospice is admitted to hospice. Not everyone qualifies for hospice. Certain criteria need to be met, most of which are set by Medicare or other payors like Medicaid or private insurance companies.

During your consultation meeting, several decisions will need to be made such as who will be the Attending Physician. Another important decision will be where the patient will reside. If the layout of the patient's current home is not conducive to caring for someone who is sick, this is the time to talk about it. One of the hardest things to give up for anyone is their home. The reality is, a decision to stay in a home which does not accommodate a change in condition can put the patient and others at risk. I have had patients who insisted on staying in their homes and put the hospice staff at risk of injury. The Hospice Team will assist you in finding the right living situation and location if needed.

Some of the most complicated and unpleasant situations for everyone involved are legal battles occurring during the last days of someone dying. It's not anyone's first choice. If you are elderly or caring for a loved one who may need hospice, consider having a legal document drawn to establish the patient's wishes. If no legal instrument is already in place and the patient is incapacitated, consider getting everyone in your family on the same page regarding medical decision making before the patient is admitted to hospice. Everyone making some compromises to establish a plan and goals can make all the difference in your family's hospice experience.

"Key" #3 - What's the Rush?

Once there is a terminal diagnosis, don't put off starting hospice care. The most common avoidable scenario I observed in my time as a Hospice Nurse was a patient who has been given a terminal diagnosis by their physician, but for whatever reason has not been admitted to hospice until just prior to their death. The definition of a terminal diagnosis in hospice care is whether a patient will likely live more than six months. For many patients and families, having hospice involved for six months, rather than six days or even six hours can make all the difference in the End of Life experience for the patient.

A common situation to illustrate this would be hospice admitting a new patient who is at a local hospital. This usually means utilizing the General Inpatient Level of Care (GIP) because they had symptoms which couldn't be controlled, such as pain or shortness of breath. The patient is usually not in good shape. Quite often patients such as these are unconscious and unresponsive to stimuli. Unfortunately, they will likely die if transported back home in this condition. The emotionally difficult part of all this for me and the patient's family would be that I would barely finish my assessment to admit the patient when they would pass away. I often asked myself, "What was I really able to do for this person? They deserved more...".

I believe hospice care can be a wonderful time of transitioning from this world to the next. This is more likely to happen if the patient and family utilize the hospice services available to them. Primary Care Physicians and specialists in a hospital also manage pain and other symptoms of patients in their care, but the setting and mission of hospice is different. Hospice allows the focus to be changed from the disease the person has to a more holistic approach to their care.

In the summer of 2015, my family experienced the loss of two family members within a one month period. One involved cancer over an extended period of time and the other death was accidental. Both losses were devastating. The former could have been a much different experience for everyone involved if the reality of the situation had been recognized and hospice care could have begun months before her passing instead of a few weeks. Instead of remembering hospitals and the side effects of ineffective treatments there could have been more laughing, conversation, and opportunities to say goodbye.

I propose a change in perspective on your part. Rather than waiting for someone in the current healthcare team you are working with to "bring up" the topic of hospice, why don't you bring it up? I believe it is in the nature and also somewhat ingrained in the training of doctors and nurses who work in a general practice setting to try to do everything they can to cure their patients before End of Life topics come up. It's only when all options are exhausted when everyone involved seems to take a breath and say, "what's next?"

Admission & Assessment

Your first contact with the clinical staff will likely be with a nurse. In some larger hospice organizations, there is a full-time position of Admission Nurse. All they do is admit new patients. If the admission is happening on the weekend, it's possible you will not see this nurse again because a RNCM will be assigned to you. If a patient is being admitted during regular business hours, your RNCM will likely do the admission. He or she will complete their visit and then pass on the information collected to the rest of the Hospice Team.

During the first visit with the RN, a comprehensive assessment is made. The session usually takes one to two hours. Vital signs are measured and major bodily functions are assessed. The visit is most often non-invasive, with no blood being drawn or any other painful procedures. Many hospice patients have been in a real battle in the course of receiving treatment to regain their health. Hospice should be an oasis from the difficult path a patient and family have been on. This is a great time to get to know your nurse and share what you hope and expect from the hospice experience.

At the time of admission, see if you have recorded a recent weight for the person receiving care. Even better, if you have a record of body weights being taken in the previous year, write them down to share with the admitting nurse. If you are in a hospital prior to being discharged to hospice care, consider asking the CNA or Hospital Nurse to complete a weight measurement. Hospital beds often have scales built in, which helps if your patient cannot stand. An accurate weight is always needed and can help your admitting Hospice Nurse make a case for admission.

Once the nurse completes their assessment and

leaves, they will spend the next several hours writing out a report of what they observed during their visit and sharing the information with the rest of the team. The Medical Director or On-Call Physician will establish a primary diagnosis and will decide if the patient meets requirements for hospice admission.

It is very important to establish the condition of a person's skin upon their admission to hospice. If your admission nurse has forgotten or hasn't inspected every inch of a patient's skin, then kindly ask them to do so. Pressure sores can cause terrible pain and may develop over a period of just a few hours. Knowing if they are present or if they are developing can make all the difference in maintaining comfort.

What's next? In the days that follow, all the disciplines involved (RNCM, Social Worker, Chaplain, CNA, etc) with hospice will make visits to your home. This can be exhausting, but it is time well spent. It is also my experience that a nurse will do an additional visit within 24 hours of admission to make sure the patient is doing well.

"Key" # 4 - It's All About Comfort

Be aware of the tools hospice provides to make the hospice journey easier. Most people have never heard the term "Comfort Kit". A Comfort Kit may go by different names depending on the individual hospice. Comfort Kits usually contain a variety of medications meant to treat symptoms such as pain, shortness of breath, constipation, anxiety, and agitation. This list may be shorter or longer depending on your specific hospice. Because these kits often contain controlled substances, they are subject to important policies and laws. Your nurse should take the time to educate and explain to you the important facts about each medication included in a Comfort Kit given to you.

Why would a Comfort Kit be needed? Getting medications to treat a symptom such as pain is not an instant thing. It usually involves at least a few phone calls to the doctor and pharmacist. If it is a controlled substance, a written prescription either faxed or physically delivered to a pharmacy may be required. Often pain medication is needed in the middle of the night, which means having a pharmacy who can fill the order may be limited. Because of these complications, it's often better to have the medications onsite instead of going through what may be hours of waiting. Am I saying every hospice patient should have a Comfort Kit delivered at the time of admission? No, I'm not. I just want it to be on everyone's radar.

It is likely your admitting nurse will bring up the subject during your first visit. If they don't, you should. Having the right medication available is no small thing. That being said, there are situations when Comfort Kits are not a possibility. Assisted Living Facilities occasionally prohibit Comfort Kits from being onsite. This may be for different reasons, sometimes because they don't have a secure place to store them.

Comfort Kits contain important, but also dangerous medications if used improperly. If you have someone in your family or if there is someone who has access to your home who has an issue with abusing drugs or alcohol, let your RNCM or Social Worker know as soon as possible. There are options for storing a Comfort Kit more safely. Also, when a Comfort Kit is stored, it must be out of the reach of children.

Here are some additional tips to consider before and during the admission of a new hospice patient:

I encourage you to educate yourself because this is likely your first experience with hospice care. Learning more about a medication which you are unfamiliar with or perhaps scares you may mean a difference in the quality of comfort. For example, there is sometimes a fear involved when the hospice nurse or physician suggests using morphine. Some people associate morphine with a person dying or being pushed towards death by the medical or nursing staff. This is not true. I am not giving advice on the use of morphine, but if you are afraid of it, please get the facts first. It's a natural drug which has benefited many patients in hospice care.

Another important tip is regarding allergies. It isn't uncommon for people to think they have an allergy when they may actually not. Sometimes this means important classes of drugs are taken out as options to treat important symptoms.

Throughout my own life, Sulfa has been listed as an allergy for me. I have no idea if it is a real allergen or not. I even asked my mother and she couldn't remember if it is true. Somehow it managed to get on my medical chart when I was a kid. Because the information is not clear, I continue not to take medications with Sulfa in it. If you can provide more information about the patient's response to food and drug allergens, please pass this information along to the nurses or doctors providing your hospice care.

Regular Visits

After the admission process has been completed, everyone on the team will settle into a regular schedule of coming to see their new hospice patient. Each discipline will have their own schedule and frequency of visits. Most commonly you will see your CNA twice per week, the RNCM or LPN one to two times per week, and the Chaplain and Social Worker on a monthly basis. Your hospice may have different frequencies for these team members to visit, so I would encourage you to take written notes and even create a calendar to avoid miscommunication.

Just so you know, there are often no real set schedules for Hospice Team Members. Their work days are often unpredictable. A crisis can pop up with another patient when your nurse is only a block away from your house and they have to reschedule your appointment. They should be communicating if they are delayed. If you are in distress or pain, communicate this to anyone on the Hospice Team and they will locate someone to get you care as soon as possible. This may mean another nurse steps in to help out.

Another way you can help out your RNCM is regarding medications. It is the nurse's responsibility to check the supply of medications when they make a nursing visit. Sometimes this is overlooked, so your participation in keeping track of what is on-hand and when you are getting low on a specific medication or medications is important. Hospice is a group effort, by working together—the patient benefits.

Safety Note: There are people who insist on continuing to smoke while they are on supplemental oxygen. In some cases, they actually wear the oxygen tubing with the O2 on while they smoke. I never had the experience of having a patient who did this, but it isn't rare to hear a story of someone who blew themselves up or burned themselves to death while smoking with oxygen on or even having the tanks and oxygen tubing nearby. Oxygen and smoking are a deadly combination.

Creating a Healthy Working Relationship

When someone enters a situation in which they are not familiar, they often defer to the experts. That's a good thing in most cases. This is likely your first experience as a decision maker involved in hospice care. You are probably a hospice rookie, but you are also probably a veteran of dealing with the "ins and outs" of managing the serious illness of yourself or loved one. The knowledge and experience you've already gained is very valuable. I encourage you to be confident in what you know and to be involved in making decisions.

Asking pointed questions like "why are we using this medication?" keeps people accountable and focused. Doctors and nurses exist in a professional environment where they are often questioned by each other, so your questions are not threatening and may sometimes catch an error.

Some issues to question may not be as serious as a medication choice but are still important. Your goals for hospice care are unique and very important. No one feels exactly the way you do about how you want your hospice story to end.

Recertification Visits

Periodically, all the team members who care for the hospice patient with the exception of the CNA do recertification visits and then fill out reports which are forwarded to Medicare or other payors. Each hospice organization does this a little differently, but the basics are the same. The Hospice Team is evaluating whether your condition has changed and whether you still qualify for the hospice benefit. Occasionally, a person's condition does improve, and they are discharged from hospice care. We call this "Graduating from Hospice". If you or your loved one are discharged from hospice, please don't take it personally. Hospices who keep patients on their service who no longer qualify can be subject to severe fines and in some cases, a professional can be charged with a federal crime, most often fraud. Medicare is trying to be a good steward for the taxpayers.

If this happens to you, your Hospice Team will provide you with important legal disclosures. Read them closely and exercise your options as you see fit. Hospice under the Medicare Benefit currently provides a procedure to appeal a hospice discharging a living patient. Your opinion counts! Speak with your Hospice Team or even an outside advocate to discuss your situation. Live Hospice Discharges sometimes occur because the Hospice Team hasn't been kept in the loop of all the details of a patient's health history and/or details of what is happening with a patient on a daily basis.

If you are "Live Discharged" from hospice, the Hospice Team will want to keep in touch with you and will gladly re-admit a patient if their condition declines back to the hospice standard.

The Unexpected Visits

It is important to know that hospice is a 24/7 365 lifeline for help when you need it. There should always be someone available on the other end of the line when you call your hospice. Please don't be shy! Sometimes the issue or problem you are dealing with can be handled over the phone. Other times, a nurse or other team member will make a visit to assess the patient.

As an On-Call Hospice Nurse, I would often get a call in the middle of the night and the first words out of the person's mouth were "I'm sorry to bother you!" That was very kind of them to think about my wellbeing, but it isn't as important as the situation they were in. Hospice professionals only have a job because you have a need. They want to help! If you need to call them multiple times because things are not going well, then please do. The comfort of a patient is everyone's first duty.

"Key" # 5 - More Than a Pain

The patient's pain matters—always tell your Hospice Team if the patient is in pain, or you think they may be. Pain management is the item at the top of every Hospice Team's priority list. In many ways, it's the main reason hospice exists. We are all concerned if a patient is in pain. Getting pain under control will and should get the Hospice Team to stand on their heads if necessary. It's an "all hands on deck" situation. Everyone on the team will drop what they are doing and join-in to help the nurse and doctor get whatever is needed to control a patient's pain.

Pain is also a mysterious thing. There is not a device we can attach to a patient which will objectively measure a person's pain. In nursing school, we were taught pain can be considered a vital sign, just like blood pressure or a person's temperature. The problem is, how do we measure it? There are two typical ways to assess a patient's pain level. The first is to ask the patient to rate their own pain level. This is done by asking this phrase, "Please rate your pain on a scale from one to ten with ten being the worst possible pain." A rating of 10 should indicate excruciating pain, on the level comparable to childbirth without the benefit of an epidural.

The numeric rating scale works well if a few things are in place. First, the person must be able to accurately report that they are in pain. Many hospice patients suffer from dementia or Alzheimer's, so the progression of their disease may affect how reliable their report may be. This doesn't disqualify or discredit them, but it usually means additional objective information is needed. Quite often other changes, like heart rate, facial expression, or body position give a good indication of discomfort.

Friends and family who know the patient well should communicate with their Hospice Nurse to point out when they believe the patient is in pain. Sometimes a patient loses the ability to speak as their disease process progresses and they must depend on their caregivers and Hospice Team to understand their physical cues indicating pain. It is better for a caregiver to say something about what they think might be pain, instead of making a judgment of no pain being present, which may be incorrect. Work with your RNCM to learn more about the physical indicators of pain.

What is a "Pain Crisis"? It can most simply be defined as an episode involving intense pain. A common scenario for a Pain Crisis is that the patient is currently being treated with medication, but this medication has become insufficient for some reason.

A Pain Crisis can be best described as: a patient not responding to an increased dosage of a pain medication, resulting in an unacceptable amount of pain for the patient. Notice I didn't define it as just being about pain. A person can be in pain, which is not good. The crisis part of the equation begins when the interventions, whether they be with medication or by other means don't work and the patient continues to be in pain. That is when the doctor and nurse work together to find a solution to a Pain Crisis.

It is important to understand the time each medication takes to become effective. Each medication is unique in the manner it treats pain and the rate at which the pain begins to go away. Also affecting the rate of pain relief is whether a medication is taken orally or some other 'route', such as a cream applied to the skin or if the same medication is given in proper form directly into the bloodstream. Ask your nurse or doctor to provide this information to you about the medications which are being used or are being proposed for use.

Patients in hospice who have pain issues sometimes take two types of pain medication—the first is long-acting while the second is "as needed". In some Pain Crisis', the patient has been given their medications properly, but the medication is not working for whatever reason.

Hospice professionals are trained well in pain treatment, so a Pain Crises is rare. Unfortunately, there are situations when pain can get out of control. Sometimes it is circumstantial as in the case of a patient who lives alone and may forget to take their scheduled dose of a pain medication. Other times, the progression of a disease causes intense pain, such as when cancer invades a new area of the body.

When a hospice professional hears "Pain Crisis", the words grab their attention!

If you are in a situation where a person's pain is not being controlled for whatever reason, the phrase "I think we may have a Pain Crisis here" is the most powerful thing you can say to a Hospice Team Member. It should immediately put the entire Hospice Team into action to get the pain controlled.

Note: Please don't misuse this phrase. It should only be utilized if it truly describes your situation.

Chapter Five

What is a Natural Death?

Until I began this type of work, I had only a few experiences with extended illnesses and death. The first person I knew who died was my great-grandfather, Severo Hernandez. He had quite a life story. Severo was born in 1879 in Mexico. At a young age, he worked as a sheepherder for a wealthy family by the last name of Rosales. He fell in love with the Hacienda owner's daughter, which was not a good career move on his part. My great grandmother's parents didn't want their daughter involved with such a simple and poor young man, so the couple chose to elope and make the trip to Colorado. Grandpa was a steelworker for several years before retiring.

Severo was ninety years old when I was born. My memories of him are still clear today. We would often visit him on weekends and see him walking from his home to his favorite bar, *Jim & Mike's* in Pueblo, Colorado.

Grandpa Severo had cancer. I'm not sure of the type. His decline was fairly rapid, with him being bedbound for only a few weeks. My grandparents, parents and extended family provided his care, with no medical or hospice workers being present. It's been forty years since his death. The family saw his death as a natural and peaceful occurrence. I am hopeful it was, but unsure it would meet the standards of today. Grandpa Severo lived to the age of ninety-eight.

How do most people actually die? Well, it's not how most of us may imagine. Death has been romanticized by the movies and TV shows we have watched over the years. Quite often people in movies speak up until the moment of their last breath, giving important messages of knowledge, love, and kindness to their loved ones. Of all the deaths I have attended, I have never seen a person have any final words or goodbyes to their loved ones prior to passing. Death is much more subtle than that and disguises itself in different ways.

There are two stages in the natural process of dying. "Transitioning" and "Actively Dying".

Transition

During the Transition stage, a person begins to sleep more and eat less, there are also other changes taking place. Some are obvious, like the fact the person may now be bedridden. This is a very difficult change for most of us—it means a loss of independence as well as the need to depend on others for basic tasks such as cleaning after bowel movements and sometimes the procedure of a catheter being put in place. For many of us, even myself, these things would be a hard pill to swallow. All the things we learned as a child are slowly taken away, walking, toileting, eating on our own. We are all so independent in our lives, taking care of ourselves and not asking others to do much of anything for us. This is can be the difficult part.

Although it can be demanding, it can also be a transformative experience when people have the opportunity to begin to let go of the worries of this world and consider their mortality. Sometimes a person verbalizes their feelings at this stage in their journey towards death, but most often it is a story only told by their eyes.

Many physiological changes occur during Transitioning, especially related to eating and digestion. Even before entering this stage, a person has often been eating much less than they have in the past. This, in combination with an underlying disease, may contribute to the decline in their health. Transitioning begins in earnest when a tipping point occurs in their disease process. It is important to know that most people in Transition do not report discomfort.

What are some of the things happening in a person's body during Transitioning? For one, the body is making choices where blood should flow, and the priorities may surprise you. Our lungs and heart function are at the top of the list with other bodily functions such as digestion and cognition becoming less important.

Without a doubt, the number one thing most families struggle with is seeing their loved one eat much less or not at all. For our entire lives, eating is seen as a measure of health and rightfully so. Seeing our loved one not eat is often felt as a failure on the part of the caregiver. Especially in situations where a person has had an extended illness, the caregiver often feels as if they have failed in their duty to provide what is needed most. The truth is that food often doesn't provide healing in this situation—it can actually make things worse. As the body prioritizes its blood flow, food consumption can create problems. The most common hazard is a person aspirating, or possibly choking on food that they can no longer swallow safely. These things happen when the patient has lost their ability to swallow properly.

Last note about food. A common concern at this stage in the dying process is that the patient is starving. The physical results may resemble starving because the patient is eating very little or nothing, but every patient I have spoken to in this situation did not complain of hunger. The prioritization the body is making also appears to take away the sensation of being hungry. What is done at this point is to provide oral care which is to maintain moisture in the patient's mouth with wet swabs to avoid a dry or cottonmouth.

Actively Dying

The best indication of death approaching is when a person has gone to sleep and is now unresponsive. Most likely, they have been sleeping more and more each day. Now their sleep is continuous and they are not responding to touch or speech.

Because they are now unconscious, they cannot eat. What usually happens at this point is a change in the mood and environment of the home. It's likely the patient has been ill for an extended time and the family is very tired. The end of the Transition phase is an opportunity for everyone to reset and begin what is often a vigil at the bedside of their loved one.

Now, you will likely be getting advice from your RNCM about maintaining skin integrity as well as comfort measures. A person's skin integrity becomes more of an issue once they are bed bound because they are not able to change their physical position. This may have been the case for a while, so you may already be changing your loved one's body position often to prevent bed sores. Many hospice patients are very thin which means they only have a thin layer of skin between the skeleton and the bed. They may no longer have a significant subcutaneous fat layer. This also is why older people are often cold.

To prevent skin breakdown, Hospice Nurses love alternating air mattress which fit right on the standard size hospital bed. These mattresses have an air pump which inflates the mattress in varying ways. The alternating inflation of the bed will change the way a person's weight is distributed on the mattress, giving those areas of contact a break from carrying so much of the body's weight.

Besides not being awake or eating, the most noticeable change in a person's condition during the Active Dying Phase is in their breathing—both the rate of breathing as well as a period of no breaths. The periods of time when someone is not breathing is called apnea. These apneic periods vary in length and frequency. Apnea usually lasts 3-5 seconds at the beginning and occurs a few times each minute. As death approaches, the apnea lasts longer each time and becomes more frequent. This breathing pattern can then change into a pattern known as Cheyne Stokes—which has great variations in the rate of breathing, both slow and fast. The rate and depth of breaths will change often, interspersed with apnea. The apnea part of this process would often keep families on the edge of their seat. I've seen a person stop breathing well past a minute in length, then take a huge breath! This would repeat itself many times over the course of hours or days. The whole experience can be an emotional roller coaster for everyone present.

As medical professionals, there is very little room for humor with families and caregivers.

I have a naturally dry sense of humor, but I had enough sense to keep my mouth shut during a humorous or ironic moment. Usually a family member or even the patient would start laughing, which would get me off the hook. The real truth is laughter and humor are therapeutic for anyone involved with hospice.

One story I will share with you, which I still fondly think about, is about a patient who lived in a very unique situation. Dolores lived with a large number of family members, most of whom were present at each visit I made. They were always very kind and supportive. It seemed each of them were dependent on each other, with no one in the house seeming to be very physically or emotionally healthy. On the night I received the call about Dolores passing, I went through my normal routine of getting out the door. "Death Visits" as we call them are sometimes a juggling act of trying to get the tasks we must accomplish like calling the doctor, coroner, pharmacist, etc. before we make all these phone calls, we must confirm the person has died.

When I entered the house, the whole family was there waiting for me. I greeted each person in the family and gave them my condolences. Each one graciously received my good wishes, and I even got a hug. When I was getting the hug, out of the corner of my eye, I saw something which didn't quite fit into what was supposed to be happening. "Nah!" I thought to myself. "It couldn't be....." I could have sworn I saw her chest rise—and sure enough, it had. My dearly departed patient had not yet left. My first thought was "This is messed up"—I felt I was a butt of a joke. After all, I had just been called in the middle of the night and told a person had died. This was fueled in part by the one comment from the gallery of, "When we saw she was breathing, we thought about calling you back." The bizarre part was they didn't say anything when I came in the door like, "She's alive." It didn't take me too long before humor and empathy crept back in. The truth is the whole family was elderly and these kind folks were starving for any love or attention, even attention related to grieving. It was a humbling experience and educated me on the great need we all have for a real connection to other human beings. Mercifully for everyone involved, my dear patient passed "for real" the next day.

How long does the active phase of dying last? As a Hospice Nurse, this was the number one question I was asked by just about everyone. It is one of the more interesting things I observed in hospice care. People have an innate desire to know when death will arrive. For some, this may seem like a "dark" thing to ask—I thought so myself at times. The reality may be different. As I have mentioned before, most families are very tired from extended caregiving. It is only natural to want to know when this long journey will end.

A good Hospice Nurse will not try to answer this question in a definitive way. It's like playing Russian roulette. Giving what you think is an educated guess will most likely backfire. But saying "I don't know" isn't exactly what most people need to hear, so I would usually find a middle ground. Throughout a person's hospice journey, a good message for a family or caregiver to hear is typical time ranges which leave some room for the unexpected. I would describe it to someone as them having months, weeks, days, or possibly hours left to live.

When someone is Actively Dying, it would be outside the norm for them to survive more than one week. Typically, people who had already been eating sparsely before losing consciousness would pass in 1-3 days. A person's ability to live without nutrition seemed to be a function of their diagnosis' and their weight.

You should know there are always exceptions to the rule. In a handful of cases, I encountered people who lived extended periods of time in this condition. The longest time I knew of was 20 days. I would be misleading you if I said this wasn't very hard on everyone involved. It was for me as well. I felt like I had let everyone down by not being able to tell them it would be so long. But the combination of this person's body type and underlying disease were very unique.

I'm trying to prepare you for all the options—even outliers. I don't want you to read this book and then have an experience different hospice experience from what I described. I have personally cared for hundreds of hospice patients and also been part of Hospice Teams involved in the care of thousands of others. My experience is that the vast majority of hospice patients had peaceful and painless deaths.

Chapter Six

One Person Can't Do It (for Long)

Every patient and family has different circumstances and resources available to them for the care of a loved one. One of the most difficult situations can be when only 1 or 2 people are available to care for the person who is ill.

On the face of it, it doesn't seem like too big a task for the ratio to be one-to-one or two-to-one. How hard could it be? It can be grueling! The best analogy is taking care of an infant who doesn't sleep. A person who is very ill may require doses of medication every 1-2 hours, and may need to have their diaper changed a couple times a night. Changing a diaper on a full grown adult can be a challenge for an inexperienced family member. There is often something to do "round the clock." Laundry, cooking, cleaning, and finding time to rest yourself. This type of schedule can wipe anyone out within a couple of days.

There may be many reasons why someone is in this situation. Sometimes there is only one child in the family and the other parent has died, leaving the adult child to be the sole caregiver. Probably the most common reason for this ratio of caregiver to patient is there is only one child or friend *willing* to provide care for the patient. What? Yes, it is not unusual for able-bodied adult children to refuse to care for a sick or dying parent. There are many reasons for this, probably the most prevalent reason being a dysfunctional relationship within the family. As a nurse, there is a big temptation to take sides in a situation like this. Hearing about one person doing all the work and taking care of Mom and Dad while other capable people sit on their hands can lead to hard feelings. Every family is complicated, so I found making yourself judge and jury for what may be many decades of dysfunction or even abuse isn't fair. Believe it or not, the most common culprit in family dysfunction is the patient. They may seem very kind and sweet in their stature and demeanor. Perhaps fifty years ago they were a tyrant in their home. Maybe even being physically or emotionally abusive to their whole family. It may be this is similar to your family's story. You're the one who was hurt and you're caring for Mom or Dad now because no one else wants to. Who's to blame? Probably, no one. Abuse and dysfunction are often multi-generational. It is only recently that the professions of mental health and family therapy have evolved.

The practical reality is one person may need to be available 24/7, which may be impossible to sustain for an extended time. Sometimes that means hiring a third party to come in and help with the overnight shifts.

Your Social Worker can help you connect individuals or companies who specialize in this work. There are agencies who specialize in providing paid caregivers who can work in shifts indefinitely. Sometimes even this isn't a solution because the patient requires more skilled care around the clock. This may require placement in a nursing home. Please recognize that your Hospice Team has been through similar situations many times. Lean on them to give you options.

"Key" # 6 - Failure is Not an Option

Communication is the Key- Speak up if something isn't right.

The Term "Service Failure" may be foreign to you, but it has a unique meaning in hospice care. It usually indicates a series of missteps by one or more team members. It is a breakdown by the organization as a whole in meeting the needs and goals of a patient and their family. In the hospice world, the term Service Failure is considered a worst-case scenario. Service Failures are often made public within the organization and may mean the termination of the employees involved. This type of systematic failure merits analysis and review so it never happens again.

What would be an example of a Service Failure? It may start with something which seems small and insignificant. Let's say a patient is admitted to hospice care late on a Saturday night. The hospital bed and other equipment are delivered just before the arrival home. The problem is, the patient and caregiver were ready to leave the hospital at 10 am Saturday morning and couldn't until the delivery occurred. Evidently, the medical supply company had a problem finding the home, and they decided to do other deliveries before finally getting to the patient's house at 5 pm. This meant a relative had to wait at the house for about eight hours waiting for the delivery. Not good. It's all been a big hassle and everyone is exhausted and on edge.

Now, it's a week after a small mishap like a late delivery, and you are almost out of your anti-nausea medication. Your RNCM had noticed you were almost out of this medication during her visit on Friday afternoon. She called in the prescription to the local pharmacy for the medicine which was to be picked up at 8 pm that night by the family. Problem is they ran out of their supply of this medication, and the pharmacist didn't call your hospice to tell them. Now it's 2 am on Sunday morning and you are in the bathroom sick to your stomach. Your niece who is your caretaker just awoke to your moaning from discomfort and has called the On-Call Nurse. Now it's in the middle of the night on the weekend, and the only 24 hour pharmacy is twenty miles away. The whole thing is a hassle for everyone involved and in the process you had to go through eight hours of discomfort because a fifty cent tablet wasn't available to take.

This is a fairly benign example of a Service Failure. My purpose is not to scare you, but encourage you to set a high standard for those who care for you or your loved one during their time in hospice care. How often does something like this happen? Very rarely.

How do you stop these types of scenarios from happening? Through communication and verification. Hospice is no different from other organizations with many people and many moving parts. If something critical needs to be done, the Hospice Team needs to be on top of it by using written and verbal communication. In our example, the RNCM would have done well to let the On-Call Nurse know that a medication had been ordered and it would be picked up that night. This didn't happen because the RNCM got another call and forgot to update the nurse coming on shift at 5 pm.

Why am I presenting this to you? The best way to get everyone's attention if you are in the middle of a Service Failure and is to use the phrase 'Service Failure' to the person answering the phone at the hospice. You could say, "I am concerned we are headed for a Service Failure in this situation. What do we need to make sure it's corrected now?" This should produce results. Other Options are, "I think we are at risk of losing confidence in your organization" or, "I think you are at risk of losing our trust." These phrases will get their attention.

When a Service Failure does occur, the people affected almost automatically get access to those at the top of a hospice organization. Complain to the boss, they will listen. Please don't cry wolf and misuse this phrase-if it isn't actually a Service Failure it will be obvious to everyone involved. Service Failures are a series of missteps and missed opportunities to complete a task which usually start as something very simple, but turns into a real problem which affects the well-being of the patient. You can also help your Hospice Team by staying in the loop on what's happening and making a quick phone call if something hasn't been completed as promised. You are an important part of the Hospice Team.

"Key" # 7 You Always Have an Option

What happens if you're not happy with your hospice? Sometimes relationships just don't work, even after you have given them a second or third chance. This happens in our personal as well as professional lives and can happen in hospice as well. If things truly aren't working with your hospice provider—don't stay in a bad situation.

Sometimes the mix of personalities just doesn't work and your loved one's care or condition may suffer. Sometimes a mistake actually happens. It could be a slow response to an urgent issue or anything else vitally important to you and your family. It may be a series of small things which deteriorate your trust in the Hospice Team.

What do you do if you have lost trust in your hospice? I always think it's healthy to talk directly with the person you have an issue with. If you have done this and still feel there cannot be a working relationship, the option to transfer to another hospice organization is available through most if not all hospice payors, including Medicare. Ask your Hospice Social Worker for more information on the details of transferring to a new hospice organization.

Transferring is actually very simple—a few papers to sign and then going through essentially the same admission process with the new hospice as with the old organization. This may be a pain of sorts, but it may be preferable to being in a dysfunctional working relationship. I have worked on both sides of this situation—it is not uncommon, and I wouldn't worry about hurting anyone's feelings. It is considered part of the business part of hospice.

It's a Marathon, Not a Sprint

Often there are multiple people providing caregiving to a hospice patient. It's still a challenge. Even with a couple dedicated siblings being supported by several other family members, people get tired. It is important to give each other breaks, so everyone gets a chance to go home, shower, sleep and reconnect with their own family. The most common reason people overextend themselves is wanting to be with Mom and Dad when they take their last breath. An illustration of this is one person who is "on shift" and actively caring for Mom while many other people are in the living room waiting for something to happen. This is likely just a very loyal family wanting to support each other, but even this routine can wipe out everyone after a few days. It is important to know that no one can predict when someone will pass.

The most common extraordinary phenomenon I've witnessed was the ability of the dying to seemingly time the moment of their passing. Parents know their children very well even if the parent is now 95 years old and their "baby" is 78 years old. As parents, we know who can "handle" different situations and emotions. The miracle I witnessed on a regular basis was the kindness transmitted by a parent in leaving at the perfect time. If the person who might be most traumatized by seeing a person actually die was at the bedside, then mom would pass when that person briefly left the room. Parents love their kids and don't want them to see things which might hurt them.

Always a Healing

It isn't uncommon to hear a person who is a patient on hospice talk about wanting to be healed of their illness or disease. I was sometimes amazed at the optimism of people who held out hope in a very dire situation. As human beings, we have an innate will to live. Although I have never seen or managed care for a person who had any type of miraculous physical healing, it was an everyday experience to see good and unexpected things happen to individuals or families during a loved one's illness.

The most common situation is healing of a damaged relationship between a parent and adult child or between siblings who have been caring for an aging parent. Occasionally, there is the drama of a person trying to travel a great distance to say goodbye to a parent who they had a difficult relationship with. Most often, they make it home before their Mom or Dad die, and there was an obvious sense of reconciliation between the two people. Sometimes, the "distant" relative didn't get home in time, but the extended family showed great love to the late arriving son or daughter. The point is that the dying experience is a natural experience which offers opportunities for flawed people to heal through acts of kindness. Sometimes just a hand being held or a kiss on a cheek to say goodbye can wipe away years of tears and sorrow.

It should also be mentioned that it is possible for you to participate in a healing for someone who is dying. It is thought that our sense of hearing is kept intact until death. This may offer an opportunity for a person who is dying to process unresolved emotions about relationships, mistakes and hurts they have in their life. I encourage you to continue to speak to a person approaching death. Your words are likely healing their soul.

Chapter Seven
When Death Arrives

Many amazing things happen when a patient passes away. My best guess is that I have attended in excess of 250 deaths in my 5 years of hospice nursing. For me, it seemed most people passed at night. The most common time I would get a phone call reporting a death was around 3 am. I often thought about why this was the case. The only thing I could come up with was that this time of the night was very still and a good time for a soul to leave in peace.

When someone passes, the first phone call a family should make is to the hospice. A nurse is then dispatched to attend the death. I was always amazed at the variety of scenes I would come upon when I arrived. Most often the emotions of the family and friends were of relief and exhaustion. There is an interesting dynamic which occurs after someone passes away.

It most often happened like this: Grandma and the whole family were very close. Grandma was sick and had her hospital bed in the living room because there was more space there. She passed away early in the morning. Slowly family members began to arrive at the home and settle into the house. Soon, the home was completely filled with family and the patient still present as well. What I observed and experienced is this: life goes on! Somewhere in our design as human beings is a reflex or response to go on with our own lives when someone we love dies. In these situations, I observed joy in a grieving family as evidenced by the tears and stories they shared.

If there was one helpful thing I said to families right after their loved one's passing, it was a simple well-timed question. I would ask this: "I only had the opportunity to know your mom while she was ill and not really herself. What was she like when you grew up?" The question opened up the floodgates. The emotions which were expressed and the stories I heard were amazing and will travel with me as a long-lasting gift for the time I was involved with hospice. Please use your own version of this question to help your loved ones share the great moments and memories of your loved one.

There is a temptation for anyone involved in medicine or nursing to think of the people we care for just as patients. By asking this type of question not only after the death of someone—but also throughout the time we care for them—we gain an excellent opportunity to give the gift of a "human" experience for everyone involved. Sometimes nurses and doctors think we are very powerful and knowledgeable. The truth of the matter is that while we may be, at times, the most amazing gift we give to the people we encounter is a human connection with someone who truly cares for them.

Saying Goodbye

A great benefit of being in hospice care is that in the vast majority of cases -no one needs to call 911 when death occurs. In most situations, the Hospice Nurse will arrive and confirm the person has passed by checking for vital signs. Then, a call is made to the Attending Physician or Hospice Medical Director to get them to pronounce the death and establish a time of death. Next comes a call or fax of information to the coroner who then decides whether to "release" the patient's body to the funeral home. In five years, I never had a corner not release a body to the funeral home. Occasionally they had additional questions, but because our records were organized and good care was provided, the patient would soon be on their way. It was usually at this point in the "Death Visit" that the nurse prepared the patient's body for transport by cleaning it gently with cloth and water. This is a humbling experience where it is impossible to avoid the thought of your own mortality. If a family member is available, having them help with preparing the body can be the absolutely most heartbreaking and heartwarming experience in life. Please ask the nurse when they arrive at your home to assist with this sacred task, it will change your life.

I want to ask for your help in making sure your loved one makes a dignified exit from their residence. This message is for both families as well as hospice professionals who may be reading this book.

It is very important for someone from hospice to stay with the family of a deceased person until the funeral home arrives. This last act of respect for the deceased and their family can make the process much easier on the family. If the nurse is unable to stay, then another team member should take their place. Families depend on their nurse and other team members such as their Social Worker or Chaplain to guide them through what to expect.

There is a new dynamic when a deceased patient has just been picked up by the funeral home and the nurse is now briefly alone with the family. I learned to have all my things like my nursing bag and computer ready to leave immediately after the funeral home leaves. This is why: in a moment's time, a nurse goes from being "one of the family" to being someone who was part of a difficult and painful chapter in their lives. I came to believe this is a protective mechanism written into our DNA and psyche. I was always sincerely thanked for my work and asked also to pass along thanks to the rest of the team, but my sense was almost always people had already moved on from this episode in their lives. In a moment, I had become a relic from a past experience.

Although the Hospice Nurse completes their role after the funeral home arrives, hospice as a whole doesn't end there. Every organization will make an attempt to keep in touch with the families of patients who have passed away. This is called "Bereavement Support". It usually consists of follow-up with an occasional phone call. Sometimes it is more involved, offering services or referrals to individuals who are having difficulty in processing grief. Please take advantage of these offers of help if you are hurting from your loss.

Request from the Author

Professionals who work in hospice are amazing people and very skilled. They are often under a great deal of pressure in helping patients, families, friends, and caregivers.

I sincerely ask you to put the knowledge I have shared with you to good use. Most of what I have shared is to help you anticipate what's next in your hospice journey, but some of what I have shared may catch your Hospice Team Members slightly off guard. From time to time, you may even have to step on a few toes to get things moving in the right direction. Isn't this the case in any human endeavor? I would certainly do this to benefit someone I loved.

Hospice Team Members will stand on their heads for patients and families when asked, but they also have to budget their time and resources to take care of all the patients they are responsible for. The "key" information and other knowledge in this book should only be used in constructive and fair ways.

Whether a patient and family realize it, they become part of a larger community when they become part of hospice. The group of patients and caregivers are all sharing limited resources in the form of their Physicians, Nurses, CNA's, Social Workers, Chaplains, and the rest of their team. Please be kind, patient, and honest with each other. By working together you can all cross the finish line on this amazing journey.

Also, in the future, you may have someone ask you to give an honest opinion about the hospice you have worked with. Please be fair in your assessment. Hospices depend on this sort of word of mouth to survive in a competitive environment.

Chapter Eight
Last Thoughts....

I'm not sure if there is an upbeat and positive way to end a book about hospice and dying. Almost all of us will pass away in the manner which I have described in this book—we'll simply slip into an ever-increasing sleep, not to awake again. In the hospice world, this is considered a success, a pain and distress-free passing.

This description may seem to be poetic. It can be. My best memories of being a Hospice Nurse are of a patient taking their last breath in the embrace of a loved one. I would also ask you to consider the possibility of death in a different context.

My encouragement to anyone reading this text is to not assume you will have time to say "goodbye", "I love you", or assume that you will have the ability to say "I'm sorry" to someone you have hurt. Most likely, you will not have the capacity to anticipate the time of their passing. Consider saying the things in your heart now. Please be assured of my prayers as you embark on your journey towards a peaceful passing.

Sometimes it's the role of a nurse to get another person motivated, so let me kindly challenge you now. If you can still walk and get in a car, consider a goal which includes seeing sites and visiting places you haven't been to before. Maybe it's visiting a person you miss or seeing a Broadway Production with your sweetheart. What's on your bucket list? If you can physically do something, why not think big by creating a memory for yourself and the people you love.

My family's own personal experience involved a family member who had an extended illness at a young age. She fought for four years to find a cure, but during this time the people in her life only were able to see her as a "Cancer Patient" trying to survive, not as the active and full-of-life person we all knew her as before her illness.

Here's my last tip for you. It is a little-known fact that hospice care follows you most wherever you are (at least in the U.S.). You can travel and still receive hospice care. Your hospice provider will coordinate care if there is a hospice organization in the locale you are visiting. If you have the energy and the resources, consider going for it! Let's say you live in New York and want to go Snowboarding in the Rocky Mountains. Ask your Hospice Team to coordinate care with one of the great hospices here in Colorado. Drop me a note!—I'll grab my board and meet you at the top of the mountain!

About the Author
Derek J. Flores, RN

Derek is a Native Coloradoan, son, brother, uncle and Dad of three amazing teenagers and personal servant to one eight pound Yorkie Mix. He works as a Registered Nurse when he is not Snowboarding or Mountain Biking in his Colorful Colorado. For five years he worked with hundreds of hospice patients up and down the Front Range of Northern Colorado. Derek has found healing and solace of his own as his nursing practice continues with a focus on caring for medically fragile children and also sharing his amazing experiences as a Hospice Nurse.

You can contact him and also hear about his upcoming projects at <u>derekjflores.com</u>

Acknowledgements

Although this isn't a book on hospice written from a religious perspective, I would like to thank God for supporting me and my family during the writing process and always. I am also grateful for my three daughters (Lauren, Danielle, and Sierra) who played different roles in making the book a success as well as a professional edit from Jesse Sprague and expert formatting from Manuel Garfio. Lastly, I have some incredible friends and colleagues who have encouraged me to chase my dreams. Thanks!